GALILEO

First paperback printing 2008
First published in North America in 2005 by the
National Geographic Society
1145 17th Street N.W.
Washington, D.C. 20036-4688

Paperback ISBN: 978-1-4263-0295-4
Hardcover ISBN: 978-0-7922-3656-6
Library ISBN: 978-0-7922-3657-3

Design: Tall Tree
Series editor: Miranda Smith
Project editor: Jennifer Schofield
Picture research: Caroline Wood

For Marshall Editions:
Publisher: Richard Green
Commissioning editor: Claudia Martin
Art direction: Ivo Marloh
Picture manager: Veneta Bullen
Production: Anna Pauletti

For the National Geographic Society:
Art director: Bea Jackson
Project editor: Virginia Ann Koeth

Consultant: Own Gingerich is Research Professor of Astronomy and the Hirstory of Science at the Harvard-Smithsonian Center for Astrophysics.

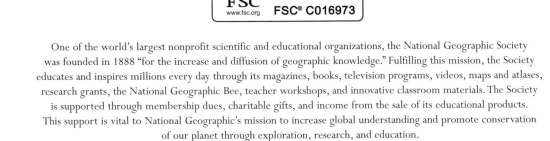

One of the world's largest nonprofit scientific and educational organizations, the National Geographic Society was founded in 1888 "for the increase and diffusion of geographic knowledge." Fulfilling this mission, the Society educates and inspires millions every day through its magazines, books, television programs, videos, maps and atlases, research grants, the National Geographic Bee, teacher workshops, and innovative classroom materials. The Society is supported through membership dues, charitable gifts, and income from the sale of its educational products. This support is vital to National Geographic's mission to increase global understanding and promote conservation of our planet through exploration, research, and education.

For more information, please call 1-800-NGS LINE (647-5463) or write to the following address:

NATIONAL GEOGRAPHIC SOCIETY
1145 17th Street N.W.
Washington, D.C. 20036-4688 U.S.A.

Visit the Society's Web site at www.nationalgeographic.com.

Previous page: Galileo's telescopes, with which he studied the moon and stars.
Opposite: A painting of Perugia shows a typical Italian street scene in the age of Galileo. Italy was a thriving center of commerce.

Printed in China
21/QED/2

GALILEO

THE GENIUS WHO CHARTED THE UNIVERSE

PHILIP STEELE

NATIONAL GEOGRAPHIC

WASHINGTON, D.C.

CONTENTS

GALILEO'S CHILDHOOD

1

STUDENT AND TEACHER

2

INQUISITION

3

THE FINAL YEARS

4

GALILEO'S CHILDHOOD

I

A Scientist is Born

It was the end of a cold winter in the year 1564. People in northern Italy were looking forward to the first spring sunshine. Wildflowers would soon be growing in the green countryside of the Arno Valley. Giulia degli Ammannati had a special reason to be happy. Her first son had been born on February 15, and now he lay fast asleep in his wooden cradle beneath the shuttered window.

His name, Galileo Galilei, had been the idea of her husband, Vincenzio Galilei, who was 18 years older than she. Vincenzio's family was very proud of its history and it was one of the family ancestors, Galileo Buonaiuti, who had first carried the name. Galileo Buonaiuti had been a doctor of medicine in the city of Florence in the 1400s.

Previous page: Galileo was born near the town of Pisa. Its famous "Leaning Tower" was built between 1173 and 1360. It is 180 feet tall and currently leans over at an angle of about 10 degrees.

Left: The birth of Galileo Galilei was registered in Pisa in February 1564. At the time, the new year was sometimes reckoned to start in March, so some records say he was born in 1563.

1543
Nicolaus Copernicus publishes new ideas about the sun and the Earth.

February 15, 1564
Galileo Galilei is born near Pisa, Italy.

Left: A boy wearing a wreath of vine leaves plays a flute. Galileo's father taught his son to play music at an early age.

All wrapped up

In the days before modern medicine, many newborn babies did not survive. To keep them healthy, it was the custom to swaddle (wrap up) babies in very tight clothes or bands. This was meant to keep their limbs straight and to prevent them from catching a chill.

He had become so famous that the whole family had taken the name Galilei in his honor. It was quite common for a first-born son to also be given the father's family name as a first name. Perhaps the family thought that this little boy would follow in his ancestor's footsteps and also become a famous doctor.

The Galilei family was not rich, but it was well respected in society. Giulia was originally from Pescia, and her husband came from Florence. Now they were living just outside the town of Pisa, in the region of Tuscany, about six miles from the mouth of the River Arno.

February 18, 1564

The great Italian painter Michelangelo dies in Florence, Italy.

April 23, 1564

The playwright William Shakespeare is born in England.

Galileo's place of birth was beautiful. Pisa had once been a wealthy and powerful city and it still had riverside palaces and fine squares. The cathedral was exactly 500 years old and the university dated back to 1338. By the time Galileo was a boy, the River Arno had become so muddy that it was hard for ships to sail up it. As a result, the number of people living in Pisa had fallen by half.

The Galilei house at Pisa was often filled with music. Galileo's father, Vincenzio, played the lute. This stringed instrument was by far the most popular in Europe at the time, and lute players were much in demand at royal courts. Vincenzio had a fine voice and was also a successful teacher, sometimes working in his home. He was very interested in the science of music, studying the ways in which strings made sounds.

Right: A lute player (left) accompanies other musicians in a small concert. The lute was played in public performances as well as in the home.

1569

Cosimo I de' Medici, Duke of Florence, is made Grand Duke of Tuscany.

1572

Galileo's parents move to Florence, but he remains in Pisa.

The leaning tower

The building of Pisa's most famous landmark began in 1173. It was a beautiful bell tower. But unfortunately, it was built on sand. The tower began to lean over before it was even finished—and it is still leaning today.

Vincenzio taught his son to play the lute, and Galileo continued to play all his life. As the boy grew older, he helped his father. Through Vincenzio's musical experiments, Galileo may have first developed his own interest in science.

In 1572, when Galileo was eight years old, his father and mother moved to Florence. It was decided that while they settled in, Galileo would remain in Pisa at the house of a relative of his mother's, Muzio Tedaldi. He was ten years old before he finally joined his mother and father in Florence.

Galileo's father's new life in Florence was very busy. Vincenzio loved to challenge people's thoughts and ideas about music, and he was forever arguing, writing, and debating—just as his son would when he grew up. Vincenzio and his friends studied ancient Greek music and drama, and it was their interest in combining the two that eventually led to a new kind of musical performance called opera.

Right: Young Galileo would have enjoyed all sorts of games. In this town square, crowds have gathered to watch soccer players scramble for the ball.

May 8, 1573
Galileo's sister Virginia is born.

1574
Galileo travels across Tuscany to Florence to join his family.

Going to School

The Galilei family was growing. During the 1570s, Giulia gave birth to two sons and three, or possibly four, daughters. The sound of music in the house was often interrupted by the noise of small children. Sadly, three of the children died young, something that happened often in those days.

In his new home in Florence, young Galileo received schooling from a private tutor. Then, when he was nearly thirteen years old, he was sent away to study at the monastery school of Vallombrosa. Set in wooded hills about 18 miles to the southeast of Florence, the school was a good place to escape the crowded city, particularly during the heat of the summer.

Right: Young Galileo's first sight of Florence in 1574 would have been the distant dome of its cathedral, Santa Maria del Fiore, also known as the Duomo.

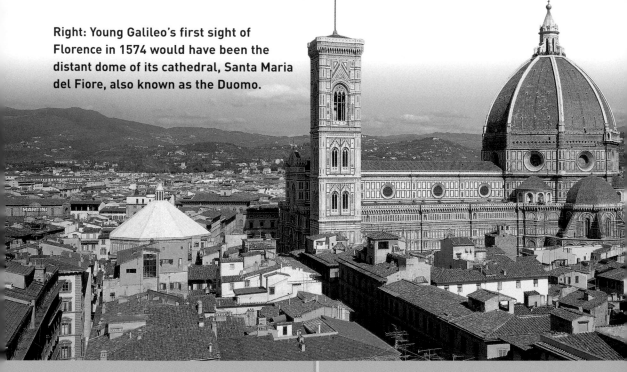

December 18, 1575
Galileo's younger brother, Michelangelo, is born.

1576
Danish astronomer Tycho Brahe builds an observatory.

Left: Galileo studied at the monastery of Vallombrosa, shown here. In southern Europe, the Roman Catholic Church played an important part in schooling.

Galileo enjoyed the strict routine of prayer, worship, and study. He decided that he wanted to become a monk, but his father was unhappy with that idea. Apart from anything else, the Galilei family would need some money coming in when the boy grew up—and monks had no income.

So Vincenzio told the monks at Vallombrosa that Galileo needed treatment for an eye problem, and brought him back to Florence. There, Galileo was sent to another school. This was also run by monks, but now Galileo was encouraged to forget the idea of becoming a monk himself.

Galileo was clever, and not just at his school lessons. He was also very good at finding out how things around him worked, inventing and making things, and drawing. He seemed to look at the world in his own particular way.

Learning languages

Galileo studied Latin and Greek. Latin was still used all over Europe as the language of science and learning. When he grew up, Galileo also wrote in the Italian of his day.

1576
Galileo is sent away to study at the monastery of Vallombrosa.

1576
The great painter Titian dies of the plague in Venice.

Italy in Galileo's Time

Italy today is a single country. During Galileo's lifetime, it was made up of small, separate states. One of these was named Florence, after its chief town. Florence had captured Galileo's birthplace, Pisa, in 1509, and in 1555 it also took over the Republic of Siena. By 1569, Florence's ruler, Cosimo I de' Medici, had been given the title Grand Duke of Tuscany. The Republic of Venice ruled northeastern Italy and other lands around the Mediterranean Sea. In Rome, the pope was the head of the Catholic Church and so was one of the most powerful people in Europe.

- City
— State boundary

SAVOY
MILAN
SALUZZO
MONTFERRAT
GENOA
Milan
Parma
Genoa
Lucca
LUCCA
Pisa
TUSCANY
Siena

VENETIA
Verona
Mantua
MANTUA
Venice
Padua
FERRARA
MODENA
Bologna
Pescia
Florence
Rimini
Urbino
Assisi

REPUBLIC

N
W   E
S

CORSICA
(of Genoa)

PAPAL STATES

Adriatic
Sea

Rome
Ostia

SARDINIA

KINGDOM
OF
NAPLES

Naples

Tyrrhenian Sea

Mediterranean Sea

SICILY

Below: Cosimo I, ruler of Florence, and all his followers enter the city of Siena. This picture is dated 1561, three years before Galileo's birth.

Right: Cosimo I de' Medici became Duke of Florence in 1537 and Grand Duke of Tuscany in 1569. He was followed by Ferdinando I in 1587, and by Cosimo II in 1609.

IO ASCHAREL IACOMO VENTVR

Everyday Life

Florence was a large, exciting city for Galileo to grow up in. There were splendid churches whose bells rang out across the city. There were palaces belonging to the richest families, and the old city hall, the Palazzo Vecchio. Above the rooftops rose the massive dome of the cathedral, the Duomo.

Above: Donkeys, bales of goods, servants, merchants, ladies, and maids—busy street scenes like this would have been very familiar to the young Galileo.

The young Galileo would have dressed each morning in knee-length woollen breeches and a simple linen shirt that were stored in a wooden chest. In the 1580s, his father's best clothes would have included a broad-brimmed hat and a long cape. Under this, Vincenzio would have worn a tunic with linen collar and cuffs, baggy breeches gathered at the knee, hose (stockings), and shoes or riding boots.

A young lady at the duke's court might wear high-heeled shoes and a long, full-skirted dress.

1577

The painter who became known as El Greco moves from Venice to Spain.

October 7, 1578

Galileo's sister Livia is born in Florence.

This would have a lacy collar called a ruff, and fancy sleeves. A fine net decorated with pearls would have been worn over her hair. Galileo's mother, however, would have worn a more simple dress with a plain collar.

Working men often wore shirts of coarse linen with the sleeves rolled up and their hose rolled up to the knee. Some wore a long apron below the waist to cover their clothes while they heaved, hammered, and sawed.

Maidservants would wear simple dresses made from homespun wool, with a linen apron and cap.

Italian ice cream

Florence was not only famous for its artists and scientists, but also for its ice cream. The first recipe for ice cream was invented by an architect called Bernardo Buontalenti (1526–1608).

Right: Two Italian peasants dressed in ragged clothes pass the time by playing the old game of "morra," known today as "rock, paper, scissors."

1578
William Harvey, who will discover how blood passes around the body, is born.

The food the maidservant placed on the table for dinner might include chicken or sausage; songbirds, such as thrushes; fish or wild duck; or hare or boar that had been hunted in the woods. A simple meal might be soup with a bread roll, cheese, walnuts, and pears or grapes, washed down with a pitcher of cool water from the well or some local red wine. Honey was used to sweeten many dishes, and spices were very popular with those families, like Galileo's, who were rich enough to afford them.

In Florence, Galileo would have seen big warehouses, shops, and street markets with sellers calling out to the passersby. There were sellers of cloth, hats, and shoes, butchers and bakers, tailors and jewellers, potters, carpenters, and smiths. The city also produced its own coins. The Medici family, who ruled Florence and all Tuscany, had made its fortune in banking.

Left: The town of Impruneta, just to the south of Florence, was famous for its pottery, its pilgrims, and its fair held each year on Saint Luke's Day (October 18).

1579
The Dutch Republic is founded in the Netherlands.

1580
Spain and Portugal are united as a single country.

Left: A hungry man sits down to enjoy his dinner—beans, bread, scallions, and meat washed down with a glass of red wine.

What did the future hold for Galileo? His mother might have thought that he would make a good businessman because her family had made its money in the cloth trade. His father was sure that he should become a doctor of medicine, following in the footsteps of Galileo Buonaiuti. That was a job that paid very well indeed.

This was a time when doctors were just beginning to find out about the human body and how it works. However, people still did not understand anything about germs and the causes of sickness. Many of the medicines available from the apothecaries (pharmacists) did more harm than good.

The greatest fear of rich and poor, young and old, was that they would catch the plague. Nobody yet knew how the plague was spread, but in fact it was passed on to humans by rat fleas—and Italian cities certainly had large numbers of rats. In plague-free years, people thanked God for their good fortune in churches, and celebrated holy days (or "holidays") with fairs, parades, and processions.

Foreign foods

People in Europe had only discovered that the Americas existed in 1492. During the 1500s and 1600s, exciting new foods began to be imported from this New World. One of the most popular new foods in Italy was the tomato.

1580

The great architect Andrea di Pietro, known as Palladio, dies in Venice.

STUDENT AND TEACHER

2

The Student

Previous page: This engraving of Galileo shows him at about 40 years old.

Above: Galileo worked very hard as a student at Pisa university, but not at medicine as he was supposed to. Instead, it was mathematics that really excited him.

It was 1581 and summer was over. Galileo was 17 years old. He had returned to Pisa, his childhood home, to study at the university. For the next four years, Galileo stayed in that city with relatives, and returned to Florence to see his family only for the summer holidays.

Young men traveled from all over Europe to study in Italy. It must have been exciting for Galileo to meet foreign students and to stay up playing cards and arguing about religion and science.

Vincenzio still wanted Galileo to study medicine, so he did. Galileo learned all the old theories about the human body and diseases. Many of these ideas were not based on science. Galileo, like his father, questioned ideas that everyone else took for granted.

Autumn 1582

Galileo goes to Pisa university to study medicine.

1582

Pope Gregory XIII brings in a new calendar. Ten days are removed from the 1582 calendar, so Easter will fall at the right time.

"Philosophy is written in this grand book the universe, which stands continually open to our gaze. But the book cannot be understood unless one first learns to comprehend the language and read the alphabet in which it is composed. It is written in the language of mathematics…"

Galileo on the importance of studying mathematics

What really interested Galileo, though, was not medicine—it was mathematics. In his second year at university, he went to a public lecture about geometry, the mathematics of shape and space. The lecture was given by Ostilio Ricci, chief mathematician to the Grand Duke of Tuscany. Galileo was inspired. He began to study the subject and discuss it with Ricci, who soon realized that this was no ordinary young man.

The "Wrangler"

Young Galileo soon made a name for himself at Pisa university. His nickname was the "Wrangler" ("Contenditore"). A wrangler is someone who loves to argue, debate, and disagree. Galileo continued to be a wrangler throughout his life.

In the summer of 1583, Ricci visited the Galilei household in Florence. He tried to persuade Vincenzio to let his son specialize in mathematics. But Vincenzio insisted that Galileo should stick with his medical studies. However, when Galileo left university in 1585, he had not completed his medical degree.

Summer 1583
The mathematician Ostilio Ricci visits the Galilei home in Florence.

1585
Galileo leaves Pisa university without his degree in medicine.

The Teacher

Galileo returned to the family home in Florence. There, he helped his father with the math for his musical experiments. He also eagerly continued his own studies in mathematics. To make some money, he taught mathematics to pupils in Florence and also in Siena. He gave public lectures on geometry and published his first book.

Below: A procession winds through the center of Siena, where Galileo taught. He always enjoyed teaching and was a popular lecturer.

In 1588, Galileo applied for a job at Bologna university. Although he did not get it, he was beginning to impress important people. One of these was a nobleman called Guidobaldo del Monte, a student of mechanics, or the way things work. Del Monte became a personal friend. Another supporter was a priest called Christopher Clavius.

1585
Galileo returns to Florence and teaches mathematics.

1587
Galileo visits the Jesuit College in Rome.

Left: This carving shows a professor at Bologna university with his pupils. Galileo sometimes found the old-fashioned university rules hard. He even refused to wear the proper robes for his job as professor.

Clavius was a very gifted mathematician. He belonged to an order of monks called Jesuits, and Galileo had visited their college in Rome in 1587. The two men wrote to each other for many years.

In 1589, Galileo was offered a job at the University of Pisa as Professor of Mathematics. The job was not well paid, but Galileo enjoyed the company of some of the other teachers there. He was interested in learning about many different subjects, from science and art to poetry and music.

In 1591, Galileo's father Vincenzio died, at the age of 71. He was buried in Florence at the Church of Santa Croce. This was a time for Galileo to think about the future. As the eldest son, he was now responsible for the whole Galilei family.

A bad start

Galileo's career as a university teacher got off to a bad start. He could not get to the first lectures he was supposed to give because the River Arno had flooded the city. Even though it was not his fault, the university cut his pay.

1588
Galileo applies for a job at Bologna university but fails to get it.

1589
Galileo returns to Pisa university as a professor of mathematics.

New Ideas

Luckily, in 1592 Galileo found a new job, and it was well paid. He was made Professor of Mathematics at Padua, the university for the Republic of Venice. The years at Padua, teaching students geometry, would be the happiest of Galileo's life. However, he often met with other professors who found him too pushy and too full of shocking new ideas.

While still at Pisa, Galileo had become especially interested in the way objects fell through the air. He was sure that all objects fell to the ground at the same speed. Most people at the time thought that heavier objects fell more quickly—after all, that was what the Greek thinker Aristotle had claimed centuries before. Today we know that Galileo was right. Air might slow down a feather more than a ball, but similarly shaped objects will hit the ground at the same time. It was said that Galileo proved this by dropping cannonballs of different weights off Pisa's Leaning Tower.

Above: Coins were carried in leather purses in Galileo's time. Galileo earned three times as much at Padua as he had at Pisa. He was eager to make money, but had to spend much of it on his family. He was always generous.

1591	1592
Galileo's father, the musician Vincenzio Galilei, dies in Florence.	Galileo becomes professor of mathematics at Padua university.

Pocket calculator

Galileo loved inventing things. In 1597, he made a contraption called a "geometric and military compass." This was made up of two folding rulers with scales. When opened out, they could be used to make calculations.

It is not known for sure whether he really did this, but in 1612, some squabbling professors who disagreed with Galileo did try out the experiment. They still refused to believe his theory, despite the evidence.

From about 1595 onward, Galileo became more and more interested in the movement of the Earth, oceans and tides, the planets, stars, and the sun.

He began to think about the ideas of the Polish astronomer Nicolaus Copernicus. More than 50 years earlier, Copernicus had claimed that the Earth was not the center of the universe but that it traveled around the sun. The great Danish astronomer, Tycho Brahe, did not think it did. However, a German astronomer called Johannes Kepler had just written a book saying that Copernicus had been right. In 1597, Galileo wrote to Kepler, saying that he was himself thinking along the same lines.

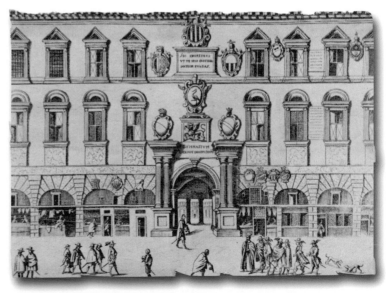

Right: Padua university (right) was one of the best universities in Europe. Copernicus had studied medicine there, from 1501 to 1503.

1597
Galileo invents his "geometric and military compass."

1597
Galileo writes to Kepler, saying that he too supports Copernicus's theory that Earth moves around the sun.

An Eye on the Heavens

During the Middle Ages, people had invented lenses: curved pieces of glass that made objects seem bigger when you looked through them. At first, these lenses were used to make magnifying glasses. Then they were used in the first eyeglasses. Some Dutch glasses-makers experimented with combining two lenses to make distant objects seem much closer. In October 1608, Dutchman Hans Lippershey gave a demonstration of two lenses mounted in a tube. This *perspicillum*, or telescope, caused great excitement across Europe. Galileo heard about it in Venice in the summer of 1609, and immediately set to work. He learned how to grind and polish lenses using the finest glass. Galileo managed to improve the magnification from three times to twenty times. The government in Venice was delighted and rewarded him handsomely. They were thinking how useful these telescopes would be for sailors and soldiers. But the young Galileo had other ideas—he turned his telescope to the stars.

Left: Galileo's telescopes made it possible to see the moon, planets, and stars clearly for the first time.

Left: Before 1608, astronomers used all sorts of different instruments to measure the movements of the sun and planets across the sky, as seen here. The telescope turned out to be the most useful invention ever for this purpose.

Above: In 1609, Galileo demonstrated his telescope to officials of the government of the Republic of Venice. They were astonished to be able to see distant ships quite clearly.

Family Matters

To enjoy himself, Galileo often traveled from Padua to Venice, the chief city of the Republic of Venice. It was a beautiful, exciting place with so many canals that people traveled everywhere by boat. It was there that Galileo met Marina Gamba, an attractive young woman 14 years younger than he was.

Above: Galileo dearly loved his daughter Virginia, who became a nun with the name Sister Maria Celeste. They sent letters to each other all their lives. She was an intelligent woman with a love of music.

By 1600, Marina was expecting a baby, and she moved from Venice to Padua to be near Galileo. On August 13, she gave birth to a little girl, whom they called Virginia. A second daughter, Livia, followed in 1601. In 1606 came a son, named Vincenzio after Galileo's father.

Galileo and Marina were not of the same social class and never married. Instead, they lived separately in Padua, he in his professor's house on the Borgo del Vignali, she in a small house on the Ponte Corvo. They were happy in each other's company, despite the fact that Galileo's mother, Giulia, disapproved of Marina.

1600
Marina Gambia gives birth to Galileo's first daughter, Virginia.

1601
Galileo and Marina's second daughter, Livia, is born.

Right: Life in the convent was very difficult. However, its walls protected the sisters from outside disasters, such as outbreaks of the plague. This terrible disease would kill Galileo's brother Michelangelo in Germany in 1631.

In 1609, Galileo's mother took Virginia to Florence, and Livia followed when Galileo left Padua in 1610. Young Vincenzio stayed with Marina for the time being. Galileo sent money for his son's upkeep. When Galileo left Padua, Marina married another man, named Giovanni Bartoluzzi. It was Bartoluzzi who provided Galileo with the glass for his first telescope lenses. This special glass came from the famous glassworks on the island of Murano in Venice.

It was normal for the daughters of unmarried parents to become nuns. In 1613, Galileo's daughters, still young girls, entered the convent of San Matteo at Arcetri, just outside Florence. In October 1616, Virginia became a nun, taking the name Sister Maria Celeste. The following year, Livia became Sister Arcangela.

A hard life

As nuns, Galileo's daughters had to give up all wealth. They dressed in rough, brown cloth and wore black veils. Much of their day was spent in prayer, or scrubbing, mending, embroidering, or gardening. It was a hard life, which often made Livia feel depressed.

1605
Galileo acts as tutor to Cosimo, the young Prince of Tuscany.

1606
Galileo and Marina's son, Vincenzio, is born.

Sun, Moon, and Stars

In 1609, Galileo's former pupil, Prince Cosimo de' Medici, became Grand Duke Cosimo II of Tuscany. In November of that year, Galileo first looked at the moon through a telescope. To his astonishment, he could see mountains and craters. Until that time, everyone had assumed that the surface of the moon was smooth.

In January 1610, Galileo observed the planet Jupiter and discovered four of its moons. He named them the "Medicean stars" in honor of Cosimo.

Galileo also looked at the Milky Way, the shining path that crosses the night sky, and realized that it was made up of countless individual stars. Around Saturn he saw a strange bulging shape, but could not yet see clearly enough to know that these were rings that circled the planet.

In 1610, Galileo was appointed Chief Mathematician and Philosopher to the new Grand Duke of Tuscany. He was also made Chief Mathematician to the University of Pisa.

Left: Galileo wrote about his discoveries with the telescope in a book called *Sidereus Nuncius* (*The Starry Messenger*). It was first published in Venice in March 1610.

1609
Cosimo II, Galileo's former pupil, becomes Grand Duke of Tuscany.

1609
Galileo observes craters and mountains on the moon.

It was an honorary role that did not involve teaching. Galileo left Padua for Tuscany that September, and rented a house in Florence with a roof that was ideal for star-gazing.

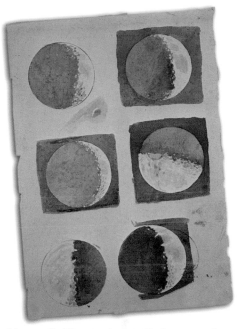

He started to observe the planet Venus. It was clear from the planet's phases (the way in which the light it reflected from the sun changed as the planet moved) that it was traveling around the sun. This was a great boost for the theories of Copernicus—if Venus moved round the sun, then so might Earth. In 1611, Galileo, visiting Rome, was proud to be made a member of the Lyncean Academy, the world's first international scientific society.

Above: Galileo took detailed notes of all his observations of the moon and the planets. Telescope images were carefully sketched.

In 1612, Galileo was joined in Florence by his six-year-old son, Vincenzio. In the same year, Galileo began to observe sunspots: the dark marks of cooler areas that appear and disappear on the face of the sun. Today, we know that these marks are caused by magnetic forces.

"In about two months, December and January, he [Galileo] made more discoveries that changed the world than anyone has ever made before or since."
Noel M. Swerdlow, 1998

1610
Galileo makes many great discoveries with his telescope, including four of Jupiter's moons.

1610
Galileo's new appointment is at the Tuscan court. He moves to Florence.

INQUISITION

3

Trouble Ahead

Galileo was a man who made friends easily. However, for some years he had been gaining enemies too. Some were jealous of his success and fame. Many were philosophers. They disliked the way in which Galileo relied on practical experiments and believed only what he saw with his own eyes. They wanted science to fit in with the fixed view they had of the universe.

Previous page: In this crayon portrait, Galileo is shown at around 60 years old.

Above: The ideas of the Polish astronomer Nicolaus Copernicus had caused furious argument for nearly 70 years. Now, as a result of Galileo's discoveries, this argument flared up again.

How did the universe work? For hundreds of years, people had accepted the ideas of the Greek thinker Aristotle, who had died in 322 B.C., and of the astronomer Ptolemy, who had died in around 170 A.D. They placed the Earth at the center of everything, and believed that the sun, moon, planets, and stars glided around it. This idea was popular with the Christian churches, too.

1611

Galileo is made a member of the Lyncean Academy in Rome, the earliest international scientific society.

1612

Galileo's son, Vincenzio, joins him in Florence.

If the Earth was God's most important creation, then it had to be at the center of the universe.

Nicolaus Copernicus, who lived from 1473 to 1543, disagreed. He claimed that the planets followed a circular path, or orbit, around the sun, spinning as they traveled. He was right,

One who got it right

Long before Copernicus' time, one astronomer noted that the Earth spins as it travels around the sun. He was a Greek called Aristarchos of Samos, who lived c.270 B.C. Nobody believed him.

although the orbits were later proved to be elliptical (oval) rather than circular. But Copernicus was mocked by many people. If the Earth really was whizzing around in this way, why couldn't they feel it? The Catholic Church banned Copernicus' book, which was called *De Revolutionibus Orbium Coelestium* (*About the Revolutions of the Heavenly Bodies*).

In 1600 an Italian called Giordano Bruno was burned alive in Rome on orders of the feared church court known as the Inquisition. He was condemned because of his religious beliefs, but he had also been a supporter of Copernicus.

No wonder Galileo was careful in what he said. However, his

discoveries were making the argument very public. Soon everybody was taking sides. Some people in the church supported Galileo, but others plotted with the philosophers to stir up trouble.

Left: This 17th-century chart puts the sun at the center of the universe, with the Earth and other planets known at the time circling around it, as described by Copernicus.

1612
Galileo begins to make detailed observations of sunspots on the face of the sun.

1613
Galileo's daughters go to live in the convent of San Matteo in Arcetri.

Galileo may have disagreed with many professors, but he really did not want a quarrel with the church. He was himself a sincere Christian. However, Galileo believed that the church should look at all the options, rather than fear them. He explained this in a letter to Benedetto Castelli, a former pupil and a keen supporter. He also explained it in a letter to the powerful Christina de Lorraine, mother of Cosimo II.

In December 1615, Galileo went to Rome, hoping to persuade church leaders to agree with him. He stayed at the Tuscan embassy, the Villa Medici. There, he wrote up his latest work on tides and the movement of the Earth. Surely, that would convince them.

However, it was all in vain. In February 1616, Pope Paul V asked a senior panel of cardinals to investigate the ideas of Copernicus. They decided that his ideas were wrong and against the teachings of the church. Galileo was ordered not to spread the ideas of Copernicus as if they were facts. This was bad news, but it could have been worse. The church confirmed that Galileo himself was in the clear.

Right: After the ban of 1616, Galileo was granted a meeting with Pope Paul V (right). The pope assured him that he was still held in respect by the church.

1616
The Inquisition declares that Copernicus' views are false, and bans them.

1617
For the sake of his health, Galileo rents a villa at Bellosguardo, outside Florence.

Left: In 1623, following the fuss about the comets, Galileo published a book called *Il Saggiatore* (*The Assayer*). In it, Galileo insisted that science must depend on experiment and proof.

Galileo's health had been poor since he had moved back to Florence. In April 1617, in need of fresh air, he rented a house at Bellosguardo, in the hills outside the city. Sometimes Galileo would walk over to Arcetri to visit the convent where his daughters were now nuns. In 1619, Marina Gambia died in Venice. Using his influence with Cosimo II, Galileo managed to get their 12-year-old son, Vincenzio, full rights under the law, even though he and Marina had never married. The following year, Galileo's elderly mother, Giulia, died.

Galileo continued to work, trying to steer clear of trouble. But, in 1618, three comets were sighted in the night sky. These caused much discussion. Galileo criticized the Jesuit astronomer Orazio Grassi for his opinions on a comet's orbit. Grassi was very offended and, as a result, he became another influential enemy of Galileo.

Torture and fire

The aim of the Roman Inquisition was to bring to trial people who disagreed with the teachings of the church. These "heretics" were tortured and burned alive. The Roman Inquisition had been founded in 1542 to fight against the opponents of the Catholics, such as those who called themselves Protestants.

1618

Observation of comets in the night sky starts a fierce debate.

1619

Marina Gambia, the mother of Galileo's children, dies in Venice.

Friends and Enemies

Arguments raged around Galileo for many years. Luckily, the scientist had many powerful supporters and friends. The Medici family, who were the rulers of Tuscany, paid Galileo's wages from 1610 onward and offered him much support. Prince Federico Cesi, the founder of the Lyncean scientific academy in Rome, was another good friend. Galileo also had supporters in the Catholic Church. The Archbishop of Siena, Ascanio Piccolomini, did all he could for the scientist. However, because the philosophers who opposed Galileo failed to win the scientific argument against him, they tried to get the church on their side. A very important church leader, Cardinal Roberto Bellarmino, was a great opponent of Copernicus' ideas. It was Bellarmino who had told Galileo of the ban of 1616, but he died in 1621. Many other churchmen, such as the Jesuit astronomer Orazio Grassi, were also very hostile to Galileo.

Above: Pope Paul V died in 1621. The next pope, Gregory XV, died only two years later. In 1623, Maffeo Barberini (above) became pope, with the title Urban VIII. Galileo knew him well. Urban VIII had long been an admirer of Galileo's work. But would he protect him from his critics?

Left: Christina de Lorraine was the wife of Ferdinando I de' Medici and grandmother of Ferdinando II (above right). She was a devout Catholic and queried some of Galileo's beliefs, but she remained supportive of him.

Right: In February 1621, Cosimo II died, aged only 30. His ten-year-old son, Ferdinando II (right), became Grand Duke of Tuscany. In the past, Galileo had taught the young prince, and Ferdinando remained friendly with the scientist into his old age.

Below: In Rome, Galileo stayed at the Villa Medici. Rome and Tuscany had separate governments, and this was the Tuscan embassy. This hospitality was the Medicis' way of showing their official support for Galileo and his theories.

The Trial

In 1624, Galileo began to write a new book. It was called the *Dialogue of the Two Principal Systems of the World*. Its aim was to contrast the ideas of Aristotle and Ptolemy with those of Copernicus. Galileo had been ordered not to put Copernicus' ideas forward as facts, so instead, his book took the form of a discussion between two people.

Galileo felt that he was on safe ground. He discussed the project in detail with leading church figures, including Pope Urban VIII himself. The book was published at last in February 1632 and was an immediate success.

There was no doubt that the argument in the book was won by the supporter of Copernicus. To some in the church, this was a step too far.

Left: This painting shows Galileo's confession being read out during his trial of 1633. The trial lasted two months, and the strain on Galileo's health was severe.

1623
Maffeo Barberini, a supporter of Galileo's work, becomes Pope Urban VIII.

1631
Galileo buys a house, called Il Gioiello, at Arcetri, near Florence.

Traveling to Rome

The ill Galileo was in no state to travel by mule or horse to Rome. Instead, thanks to the Medici family, he traveled in a litter: a carriage on poles held by strong porters. Although this allowed him to lie down, it was still a bumpy journey that took almost two weeks.

One of these was a Jesuit priest called Christopher Scheiner, who was jealous of Galileo's success. He claimed that he had found out about sunspots before Galileo. To get revenge, he stirred up feelings and spread rumors about Galileo.

These rumors reached the ears of Pope Urban VIII, Galileo's former friend. The pope was facing big political problems. The Thirty Years' War had raged across northern Europe since 1618. This was a terrible conflict between Catholics and Protestants, and the pope was being urged to take a hard line against any ideas that might challenge the Catholic faith. In the middle of all this, Urban VIII was told by Galileo's enemies that the new book insulted him and made him look stupid. He was furious.

In September 1632, sales of the new book were banned. Galileo was ordered to go to Rome to face the Inquisition. He was now an elderly man and in poor health. His doctors said he should not travel, but the church insisted. On January 20, 1633, Galileo left Arcetri to stand trial in Rome.

"I feel the Pope could not have a worse disposition to our poor Signor Galilei..."

Report by Ambassador Francesco Niccolini of Tuscany, 1632

1632

Galileo publishes *Dialogue of the Two Principal Systems of the World*.

1632

Galileo is summoned to stand trial in Rome, but is too ill to travel.

Galileo, ill and exhausted, stayed at the Villa Medici in Rome. The trial began at last on April 12, 1633 and dragged on until June 22, 1633.

The Inquisition tried to prove that Galileo had failed to clear publication of his book with the authorities. Galileo insisted that he had. He did not send an advance copy of the book to Rome, but that was because the city had been sealed off because of the plague.

He was also accused of breaking the ban of 1616 by declaring his support for Copernicus. Galileo would have none of it. The book, he said, showed both sides of the argument fairly. The final session of the trial began on June 21, and Galileo was finally found guilty of being a heretic for encouraging the belief that the Earth moved around the sun. Some of his judges disagreed and refused to sign the verdict.

Left: Santa Maria sopra Minerva, a convent and church in Rome, was the scene of Galileo's final trial and his promise to reject the teachings of Copernicus.

April 1633
Galileo goes on trial in Rome.

June 1633
Galileo is found guilty and forced to reject Copernicus.

> *"I have been judged vehemently suspected of heresy, that is, of having held and believed that the Sun is the center of the world and immovable and that the Earth is not the center and moves."*
> **Galileo as reported by Ambassador Francesco Niccolini of Tuscany, 1632**

On June 22, dressed in a white robe, Galileo knelt before the judges and promised to give up such beliefs. There is a legend that as he got to his feet, he muttered in Italian, *"Eppur si muove!"* ("But it does move!"). It would have been very dangerous for him to have said such a thing at this stage, but that must have been what he was thinking.

Galileo was sentenced to imprisonment, but his supporters pleaded for him not to be treated too harshly. He was taken back to the Tuscan embassy at the Villa Medici. Later it was agreed that he could remain under arrest at the palace of the Archbishop of Siena, his true friend Ascanio Piccolomini. There he was cared for and kept in comfort for five months.

Right: This is the title page of Galileo's book *Dialogue of the Two Principal Systems of the World.* **After the ban on its sale, it was passed out of Italy to northern Europe. This edition, in Latin, was published in Holland.**

June 1633
Galileo is sentenced and handed over to the care of the Archbishop of Siena.

August 1633
Galileo's *Dialogue* is passed out of Italy to northern Europe.

THE FINAL
YEARS

4

House Arrest

The trial left Galileo depressed and weary. The Archbishop of Siena decided that the best way to get his friend on the road back to health was to involve him in lively discussion and practical projects. The plan worked, but only up to a point. Galileo was was soon putting his mind to scientific problems once more, but his health remained poor.

Galileo's supporters, such as the Tuscan ambassador, Francesco Niccolini, pleaded for Galileo to be given his freedom, or at least sent home. At the same time, his enemies did their best to spread suspicion about Galileo's friends, even about the Archbishop of Siena.

At last, in December 1633, Galileo was allowed to go home. He returned to Il Gioiello, "The Jewel," his house at Arcetri.

Previous page:
This painting shows Galileo in his old age, six years before his death.

Right: Galileo's last years were spent in this house at Arcetri, near Florence.

December 1633
Galileo is allowed to return to his house at Arcetri, under house arrest.

April 1634
Galileo's eldest daughter, Sister Maria Celeste, dies. He is heartbroken.

Left: Galileo's mind remained as sharp as ever in his old age. His scientific theories are noted by an assistant in this picture.

Galileo remained under house arrest at Il Gioiello. He was not allowed to leave Arcetri, see friends, teach students, or publish books. However, he was welcomed home in person by Grand Duke Ferdinando II.

Sadly, Galileo's troubles were not over. At the beginning of April 1634, his daughter, Sister Maria Celeste, died at age 33. He was heartbroken. For many years, this loving and intelligent woman had written letters to her father, sent him little gifts, and prayed for him. He had always written back, and tried to help her and the convent.

For a time, relatives stayed with Galileo at Arcetri, but finally he was left alone with his grief. As always, he turned to science for comfort.

"...immense sorrow and melancholy [accompany] loss of appetite; ...I have at present no heart for writing, being quite beside myself so that I neglect even replying to the personal letters of friends."

A letter from Galileo to a friend in Florence, in 1634, after the death of his daughter

August 1634
Galileo begins to renew contact with other mathematicians.

Autumn 1634
Galileo resumes work on his last book.

What We Know Now

How did Galileo's knowledge of the sky at night compare with our own?
He found out that the planets were other worlds, which, like Earth, traveled
around the sun. The only planets he knew existed were Mercury, Venus, Mars,
Jupiter, and Saturn. However, Galileo believed that there were others out there.
Uranus was not discovered until 1781, Neptune until 1846, and Pluto until 1930.
Galileo did not know that distant stars were also suns, and that some of these had
their own planets around them. Today we know that even the sun spins as it travels
through space at about 500,000 miles per hour. There is nothing motionless in the universe.

Right: This space probe is named after Galileo. It was launched in 1989 to find out more about the planet Jupiter. In December 1995, the probe finally entered Jupiter's atmosphere.

Above:
Using one
of his telescopes,
Galileo discovered four
of Jupiter's moons. One of them, Io, was
photographed by the Galileo space probe
in 1996. Io is colored red, orange, and yellow
by its sulfur. It also has volcanic hot spots.

Right: We know now that
the strange shape Galileo
observed around the planet
Saturn was really a series of beautiful
rings. These rings are made up of billions
of pieces of ice, rocks, and dust.

Spreading the Word

Galileo's last great project had taken shape in his head while in Siena, during the months after his trial. He was thinking back to the experiments on motion that he had carried out as a young man at the universities of Pisa and Padua. He decided it was time to write a new book about these.

A swinging lantern

Galileo remembered how he had once watched a lantern swinging to and fro in Pisa's cathedral. He had noticed that it moved back and forth in equal time. However long swinging rods (or pendulums) were, the time they took to swing stayed much the same. Galileo used this discovery to design a pendulum clock. His son drew up the plans, but working pendulum clocks did not come into use until after Galileo's death.

The experiments had measured the way objects roll down slopes and gather speed. They had also examined balance and force. However, the experiments had been largely ignored by other thinkers in the universities. Galileo's new work also discussed the mathematics of structures. It had a long title: *Discourses and Mathematical Demonstrations, Concerning Two New Sciences Pertaining to Mechanics and Local Motions*. Galileo, of course, had a problem—he was still under house arrest and so forbidden to publish any new work. His supporters tried to find a way of getting around the ban. In the end, they arranged secretly for the book to be published at Leiden in Holland, a Protestant country beyond the reach of the Inquisition.

1636
Louis Elzevir agrees to publish Galileo's book in Leiden, Holland.

1637
Despite his failing eyesight, Galileo makes observations of the moon.

Although Galileo was watched closely, pages of his new book were slipped out of Arcetri in batches and taken northwards to the Dutch printer Louis Elzevir. Finally, in 1638, the book was published and was one of Galileo's greatest successes. If Galileo had not given in to the demands of the Inquisition in 1634, this work would never have been published.

In the spring of 1638, Galileo's eyesight and health were failing rapidly. He asked for permission to go into Florence to see his doctors. He was refused.

Below: This is a printing press used in the 1630s. Since the 15th century, books had no longer been copied by hand. Instead, they were printed quickly in large numbers. This made it much harder to stop books like Galileo's from reaching people.

March 1638
The church refuses to let Galileo visit his doctors in Florence.

June 1638
Galileo's new book, *Two New Sciences*, is printed.

The Fading Light

Galileo had always suffered from trouble with his eyes, and may have damaged them observing the sun. He now had glaucoma (a build-up of pressure within the eye) and cataracts (a hardening of the eye which stopped him from seeing clearly). By 1638, he was completely blind.

As Galileo himself said, it was particularly hard for a man who had seen further into space than anyone in history to suffer blindness. Beginning in 1638, he was helped by a new secretary called Vincenzio Viviani, who took notes for him, read letters, and helped in many ways. Viviani had been

suggested by the Grand Duke. He was a very intelligent young man and a great admirer of Galileo.

Galileo may have been in disgrace with the Catholic Church, but his house arrest actually resulted in his work being read all over Europe. He became very famous.

Left: Vincenzio Viviani became Galileo's secretary when he was just 17 years old. Very clever and hard-working, he was the ideal assistant. He remained an admirer of Galileo all his life.

1638
Galileo becomes completely blind.

1638
Vincenzio Viviani becomes Galileo's secretary at Arcetri.

Left: The English poet John Milton admired Galileo. When he too became blind in 1652, he must have thought back to their meeting in Italy.

The old man was not supposed to have visitors, but a number of well-known people managed to come to see him. Visitors to Galileo's home included, in 1634, the English philosopher Thomas Hobbes, who had read a version of Galileo's *Dialogue*. Another visitor, in 1639, was John Milton, the greatest English poet of his day. He mentioned Galileo and his telescope in his famous poem *Paradise Lost*.

The brilliant Italian scientist Evangelista Torricelli stayed at Il Gioiello during the final days of Galileo's life, taking down mathematical notes from the old master. Torricelli later invented the first barometer, which used mercury to record air pressure, and worked out the principles of water pumps, which we still rely on today. He also improved the working of telescopes and microscopes.

Right: When Galileo died, Evangelista Torricelli took over his job as Chief Mathematician to the Grand Duke of Tuscany.

1639
The great English poet John Milton visits Galileo.

October 1641
The scientist Evangelista Torricelli moves into Il Gioiello.

In November 1641, Galileo came down with a fever, and he became very ill during the month of December. He died on January 8, 1642, at the age of 77. Those present at his bedside included his son, Vincenzio Galilei, his secretary Vincenzio Viviani, and the scientist Evangelista Torricelli.

Grand Duke Ferdinando II wanted Galileo to be buried in a fine tomb in the church of Santa Croce in Florence, next to Galileo's father, but the pope refused permission. Instead, Galileo was buried in a small side room of one of Santa Croce's chapels. Galileo's son, Vincenzio, died in 1649, and his younger daughter, Sister Arcangela, ten years later.

Left: The marble tomb of Galileo Galilei shows him holding a telescope. On either side are statues that represent Astronomy and Geometry.

January 8, 1642

Galileo Galilei dies. He is buried in a side room at the church of Santa Croce in Florence.

1649

Vincenzio Galilei, son of Galileo, dies.

"Today news has come of the loss of Signor Galilei, which touches not just Florence but the whole world, and our whole century..."
Lucas Holste, librarian to Cardinal Francesco Barberini, 1642

Galileo's young secretary Vincenzio Viviani made a name for himself, and followed Torricelli as court mathematician in 1647. He never forgot his debt to Galileo. He collected Galileo's work and campaigned throughout his long life for the scientist to be officially honored. When Viviani died in 1703, he was buried next to Galileo.

It was not until 1737 that a grand tomb was finally erected in Galileo's honor in the main part of Santa Croce. His coffin was reburied there and remains in the church to this day. However, Galileo's great book, the *Dialogue*, was banned for Roman Catholics until 1835. In 1892, the University of Pisa awarded Galileo the degree he had failed to gain in 1585. It was not until 1992, after a 13-year debate that covered the conflict between science and faith, that Pope John Paul II formally closed the Catholic Church's case against Galileo, admitting that mistakes had been made in the trial.

A mystery coffin

When Galileo's coffin was moved to the new tomb in 1737, a second, unmarked coffin was discovered beneath it. This was believed to contain the remains of his eldest daughter, Virginia, Sister Maria Celeste. It was also placed in the new tomb.

1659
Galileo's younger daughter, Livia, Sister Arcangela, dies.

1737
A new tomb is built at Santa Croce in Galileo's honor.

After Galileo

The years after Galileo's death saw many of his theories proved. By 1657, the Dutch scientist Christiaan Huygens had observed that rings surround the planet Saturn. He had also produced a working pendulum clock. By 1687, the English astronomer Isaac Newton had worked out the laws of motion and the nature of gravity—the tugging force that holds the planets on their paths around the sun.

Above: Isaac Newton was born in 1642, the year of Galileo's death. Newton was a brilliant mathematician and scientist who shared Galileo's fascination with motion and with telescopes.

Beginning in about 1695, Edmond Halley studied comets and their paths around the sun. In 1729, another Englishman, James Bradley, published his measurements of light from the stars. These gave the first definite proof that the Earth is moving through space, just as Copernicus had said.

The make-up of the galaxy was worked out by the German philosopher Immanuel Kant in 1755. And, in 1851, French scientist Jean Bernard Léon Foucault showed that the Earth itself spins around.

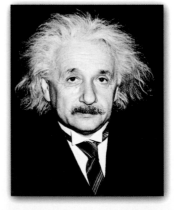

Right: Like Galileo, the scientist Albert Einstein, born in Germany in 1879, increased our understanding of the universe. Einstein believed that scientists should stand up for themselves against those in power.

1835
Galileo's *Dialogue* is taken off the Catholic Church's list of banned books.

1892
The University of Pisa awards Galileo a degree.

Right: Telescopes have come a long way since Galileo's lifetime. This picture of the Hubble Space Telescope was taken in 1999. Circling the Earth at about five miles per second, it can pick up images from the edges of the known universe.

Galileo Galilei lived in an exciting age in which modern science, mathematics, medicine, and astronomy were being born. He was someone who tried to separate science from tradition and superstition. Like many scientists today, he found himself challenged by those in power. As is frequently the case, the attempts to silence him only made his work better known.

At his trial of 1633, should Galileo have agreed to go back on his beliefs? Or should he have stood firm, even if it meant jail or death? Many people still argue over this question. However, even during his house arrest, Galileo went on to carry out further important work, and the truth—as it so often does—came out in the end.

Left: This image from the Hubble Space Telescope shows new stars being formed in the Eagle Nebula. Galileo's search for knowledge about the universe is being continued today.

1969
Neil Armstrong becomes the first man to walk on the moon.

1992
Pope John Paul II admits mistakes were made in the trial of Galileo.

Glossary

air pressure the force with which the air pushes against a surface.

ancestor somebody from whom a person is directly descended.

astronomer somebody who studies planets, moons, stars, and the workings of the universe.

barometer an instrument that is used to measure air pressure.

cardinal (of the church) a senior Roman Catholic official appointed by the pope.

cathedral the most important church in a region or town, led by a bishop.

comet a ball of dust and ice that travels around the sun; it develops a long tail of dust and vapor.

convent a building where nuns can lead a religious life.

dialogue a conversation between two people.

degree a rank given to students who have successfully completed a course at university.

edition a published version of a book.

elliptical taking the shape of a flattened circle, or oval.

embassy a group of officials looking after their home country from abroad, or the building in which these officials work.

experiment a scientific procedure that puts an idea or process to the test.

galaxy a group of many millions of stars moving through space, held together by the force of gravity.

gravity the force that pulls objects towards the Earth's center and holds planets in orbit around the sun.

heretic someone who does not hold the accepted teachings of a religion; they may often face condemnation.

hot spot an area with higher than normal temperature.

house arrest being forbidden to leave your own house or neighborhood.

Inquisition a special court set up by the Roman Catholic Church in order to consider questions of faith and morality.

Jesuit a member of the Society of Jesus, an order of monks founded in 1534.

lens a piece of transparent substance, usually glass, that may curve inwards or outwards. Lenses can be used to magnify objects.

litter a stretcher or a small carriage on poles, carried by porters.

magnification making an object seem bigger, by using a lens.

mercury a silvery metal that is liquid at room temperature.

microscope an instrument that is used to magnify very small objects.

momentum the force, or amount of motion, in a moving object.

monastery a building where monks can lead a religious life.

motion movement.

observe to watch something very carefully.

orbit the path traveled by a planet or moon around a larger object.

order a religious society of monks, nuns, or knights.

peasant a country laborer who is often very poor.

pendulum a weighted rod or cord that swings back and forth, driven by the forces of gravity and momentum.

philosopher someone who studies knowledge, truth, and logic.

pilgrim a person who travels to a holy place as a religious act.

plague a very dangerous infectious illness.

planet a world, such as the Earth, that travels around a star, such as the sun.

pope the head of the Roman Catholic Church, who lives in the Vatican, Rome.

Protestant a member of one of the Christian movements which, from the 1500s, claimed that the Roman Catholic Church was corrupt, and demanded simpler forms of worship.

publish to print and distribute a work such as a book.

Roman Catholic a member of the Christian church based at Rome.

space probe an unmanned spacecraft sent into space to explore and observe the planets, moons, and stars.

star a huge ball of gas that gives out light and heat, such as the sun.

sulfur a natural, non-metallic substance whose compounds can be very smelly.

superstition a fanciful belief, often based around luck charms and omens, that cannot be backed up by science.

sunspot one of the dark patches that appear on the face of the sun from time to time. They mark cooler parts of the sun and affect magnetism on Earth.

telescope any instrument that examines images or signals of distant objects. It is commonly a tube with two glass lenses.

theory a scientific idea; a set of proposals designed to explain a problem or a process.

thermometer an instrument designed to measure temperature.

tide the rise and fall of the oceans on Earth, caused by the gravity of the moon and the sun.

Tuscan from Tuscany, the region around Florence in Italy.

tutor a private teacher or university assistant.

universe all of space and everything that exists within it.

university an institute of higher education that offers lectures, research, and degrees.

volcanic something formed by fiery eruptions from deep inside a volcano.

Bibliography

Galileo: A Short Introduction, Drake, Srillman, published by Oxford University Press, 1996

Galileo Galilei: Inventor, Astronomer and Rebel, White, Michael, published by Blackbirch Press Inc., 1999 (originally published by Exley, 1991)

Galileo's Daughter: A Drama of Science, Faith and Love, Sobel, Dava, published by Fourth Estate, 1999

Source of quotes:

p.23 *The Assayer*, 1623, translated by Dava Sobel in *Galileo's Daughter*
p.33 Noel M. Swerdlow, "Galileo's Discoveries with the Telescope and their Evidence for the Copernican Theory," in *The Cambridge Companion to Galileo*, ed. Peter Machamer, Cambridge University Press, 1998

p.43 Report by Ambassador Francesco Niccolini of Tuscany, 1632
p.45 Report by Ambassador Francesco Niccolini of Tuscany, 1632
p.49 A letter from Galileo to a friend in Florence, 1634
p.57 Lucas Holste, Librarian to Cardinal Francesco Barberini, 1642

Some websites that will help you to explore Galileo Galilei's world:

galileo.rice.edu
www-gap.dcs.st-and.ac.uk/~history/
 Mathematicians/Galileo.html
www.galileo-galilei.org
www.law.umkc.edu/faculty/projects/ftrials/
 galileo/galileo.html

Index

Acknowledgments

Sources: AA = The Art Archive, BAL = The Bridgeman Art Library.

B = bottom, T = top.

Front cover (Galileo) The Gallery Collection/Corbis, (telescope) Gustavo Tomsich/Corbis; **1** Scala, Florence/Museo della Scienza, Florence; **3** AA/Dagli Orti; **4T** AA/Dagli Orti; **4B** Scala/HIP/British Library, London; **5T** BAL/Alinari/Biblioteca Marucelliana, Florence; **5B** AA/Dagli Orti; **7** AA/Dagli Orti; **8** Scala, Florence/San Ranierino; **9** akg-images/Erich Lessing; **10** Scala, Florence/Museo Civico, Treviso; **11** Scala, Florence/Palazzo Vecchio, Florence; **12** Scala, Florence; **13** Scala, Florence/Villa Pazzi, Prato; **15T** Scala, Florence/State Archives, Siena; **15B** BAL/Galleria degli Uffizi, Florence; **16** AA/Dagli Orti; **17** AA/Dagli Orti; **18** Scala, Florence/Galleria Palatina, Florence; **19** Scala, Florence/Galleria Colonna, Rome; **21** Scala/HIP/British Library, London; **22** akg-images/Rabatti-Dominigie; **24** Corbis/© Archivo Iconografico, S.A.; **25** Scala, Florence/Museo Civico, Bologna; **26** BAL/Bargello, Florence; **27** Science Photo Library; **28** Scala, Florence/Museo della Scienza, Florence; **28–29, 29T** akg-images; **29B** Scala, Florence/Tribuna di Galileo, Florence; **30** BAL/Alinari/Torre del Gallo, Florence; **31** AA/Dagli Orti; **32** Scala/HIP/National Museum of Science and Industry, London; **33** Scala, Florence/Biblioteca Nazionale, Florence; **35** BAL/Alinari/Biblioteca Marucelliana, Florence; **36** AA/Dagli Orti; **37** Corbis/© Bettmann; **38** Scala, Florence/Private Coll., Lucca; **39** Scala/HIP/National Museum of Science and Industry, London; **40T** Scala, Florence/Private Coll., Florence; **40B** akg-images/Rabatti-Dominigie; **41T** BAL/Museo degli Argenti, Palazzo Pitti, Florence; **41B** Scala, Florence; **42** BAL/Private Collection; **44** Scala, Florence; **45** BAL/Bibliotheque Nationale, Paris; **47** AA/Dagli Orti; **48** Scala, Florence/Museo di Firenze com'era, Florence; **49** AA/Dagli Orti; **50** Science Photo Library/US Naval Observatory; **51T** Science Photo Library/NASA; **51B** Science Photo Library/NASA; **53** akg-images; **54** BAL/Alinari/Galleria degli Uffizi, Florence; **55T** Getty Images/Hulton Archive; **55B** Scala, Florence/Galleria degli Uffizi, Florence; **56** BAL/Santa Croce, Florence; **58T** Scala, Florence/Galleria degli Uffizi, Florence; **58B** Corbis/© Bettmann; **59T** Science Photo Library/NASA; **59B** Science Photo Library/Space Telescope Science Institute/NASA.